W9-CIP-033

CHAMPION
SOCCER CLUBS

REAL MADRID

SOCCER CHAMPIONS

JEFF SAVAGE

LERNER PUBLICATIONS ◆ MINNEAPOLIS

Copyright © 2019 by Lerner Publishing Group, Inc.

All rights reserved. International copyright secured. No part of this book may be reproduced, stored in a retrieval system, or transmitted in any form or by any means—electronic, mechanical, photocopying, recording, or otherwise— without the prior written permission of Lerner Publishing Group, Inc., except for the inclusion of brief quotations in an acknowledged review.

Lerner Publications Company
A division of Lerner Publishing Group, Inc.
241 First Avenue North
Minneapolis, MN 55401 USA

For reading levels and more information, look up this title at www.lernerbooks.com.

Main body text set in Adrianna Regular.
Typeface provided by Chank.

Library of Congress Cataloging-in-Publication Data

Names: Savage, Jeff, 1961– author.
Title: Real Madrid : soccer champions / Jeff Savage.
Description: Minneapolis : Lerner Publications, 2018. | Series: Champion soccer clubs | Includes bibliographical references and index. | Audience: Age 7–11. | Audience: Grade 4 to 6.
Identifiers: LCCN 2017050964 (print) | LCCN 2017050328 (ebook) | ISBN 9781541525528 (eb pdf) | ISBN 9781541519862 (lb : alk. paper) | ISBN 9781541527959 (pb : alk. paper)
Subjects: LCSH: Real Madrid Club de Fútbol—History—Juvenile literature.
Classification: LCC GV943.6.R35 (print) | LCC GV943.6.R35 S28 2018 (ebook) | DDC 796.334/64094641—dc23

LC record available at https://lccn.loc.gov/2017050964

Manufactured in the United States of America
1-44322-34568-1/25/2018

CONTENTS

INTRODUCTION
REAL HEROES

Real Madrid was on the attack. Cristiano Ronaldo flicked a pass to Dani Carvajal, who passed it right back. Ronaldo blasted the ball. It flew past three defenders and into the net! Real Madrid had a 1–0 lead.

The team was playing Italy's Juventus in the 2017 **Champions League** final match. More than 65,000 people filled the stadium. Real Madrid fans cheered and celebrated when Ronaldo scored. They loved to see their heroes perform their magic.

In 2017, sports network ESPN named Cristiano Ronaldo the most famous athlete in the world.

Dani Carvajal (*bottom*) helped Real Madrid with smart passes and tough defense.

Juventus responded. Mario Mandzukic had his back to the goal. He kicked the ball backward over his head. Amazingly, the shot went in to tie the score.

After winning the Champions League in 2016, Real was trying to become the first back-to-back champion in 25 years. In 12 previous Champions League games that season, Real Madrid had scored 32 goals. But the Juventus defense was fierce. They had allowed just three goals in their 12 games.

The 2017 Champions League final match took place in Cardiff, Wales. The next day, Real Madrid players showed their fans the championship trophy from a bus in Madrid.

Madrid's Carlos Henrique Casemiro kicked a long shot in the second half. The ball bounced off a defender and spun into the goal. Three minutes later, Carvajal sent a pass to Luka Modric. Modric **centered** the ball to Ronaldo, who knocked it in for a 3–1 lead.

Madrid **midfielder** Marco Asensio tapped in a goal to close out a 4–1 victory. "It's not easy to score four goals against Juventus," said Real coach Zinedine Zidane. "I almost feel like dancing."

Ronaldo became the Champions League's top scorer for the fifth year in a row in 2017.

CREATING A WINNER

In the late 1800s, a group of men gathered every Sunday in a field in Madrid, Spain, to play soccer. Among them were Julian Palacios and brothers Juan and Carlos Padros. In 1902, they decided to form an official team. They named it Madrid Club de Futbol (CF), or Madrid Football Club. People call the sport football in most places outside the United States.

That year, the three leaders of Madrid CF started a national tournament in honor of the king of Spain. They called it Copa del Rey (King's Cup). Five Spanish teams competed. Madrid lost in the final match. But starting in 1905, Madrid won four straight Copa del Rey titles.

For a decade, the team played its matches at various sites. In 1912, Madrid started playing at Campo de O'Donnell. The stadium held 5,000 fans. King Alfonso XIII granted the team the title Real (royal) in 1920. They became Real Madrid CF. Four years later, the team moved into Estadio

SIDELINE REPORT

Real Madrid's logo shows the letters *MCF* for Madrid Club de Futbol. A crown was added to the logo in 1920 when the king of Spain granted the team their royal title.

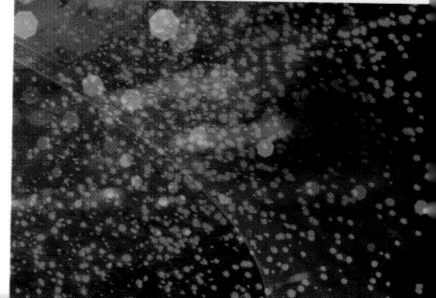

Fans stand on the edges of a field in 190 to watch Madrid play.

Chamartin, a 22,500-seat stadium.

In 1929, Real was among 10 teams in Spain to form **La Liga**. Real lost the championship game that year to Football Club (FC) Barcelona. Madrid won the La Liga title in 1932 and repeated as champions the next year. Then they won the Copa del Rey in 1934 and 1936.

Real was enjoying incredible success. But just one month after their Copa del Rey victory in 1936, war broke out in Spain. Soccer in the nation halted as the Spanish Civil War (1936–1939) raged. When play resumed after the war, many Real Madrid players had retired or left the country. Santiago Bernabeu had played for 16 years for Real. He became club president in 1943 and helped rebuild the team.

Real Madrid faced FC Barcelona in the 1943 Copa del Rey. The teams would play two games, and the team with the better combined score would advance in the tournament. Real lost to FC Barcelona, 3–0, in

Santiago Bernabeu

Real Madrid player
1957 after the t

Soldiers march during the Spanish Civil War. Hundreds of thousands of people died fighting for control of the country.

the first game. In the second match, Real won by an astounding score of 11–1. The two teams had formed a great **rivalry**.

Four years later, Real built a new stadium in Madrid called New Chamartin Stadium. In 1955, the team renamed it Santiago Bernabeu Stadium. With a history of success and a new place to play, Real Madrid was ready to become a **dynasty**.

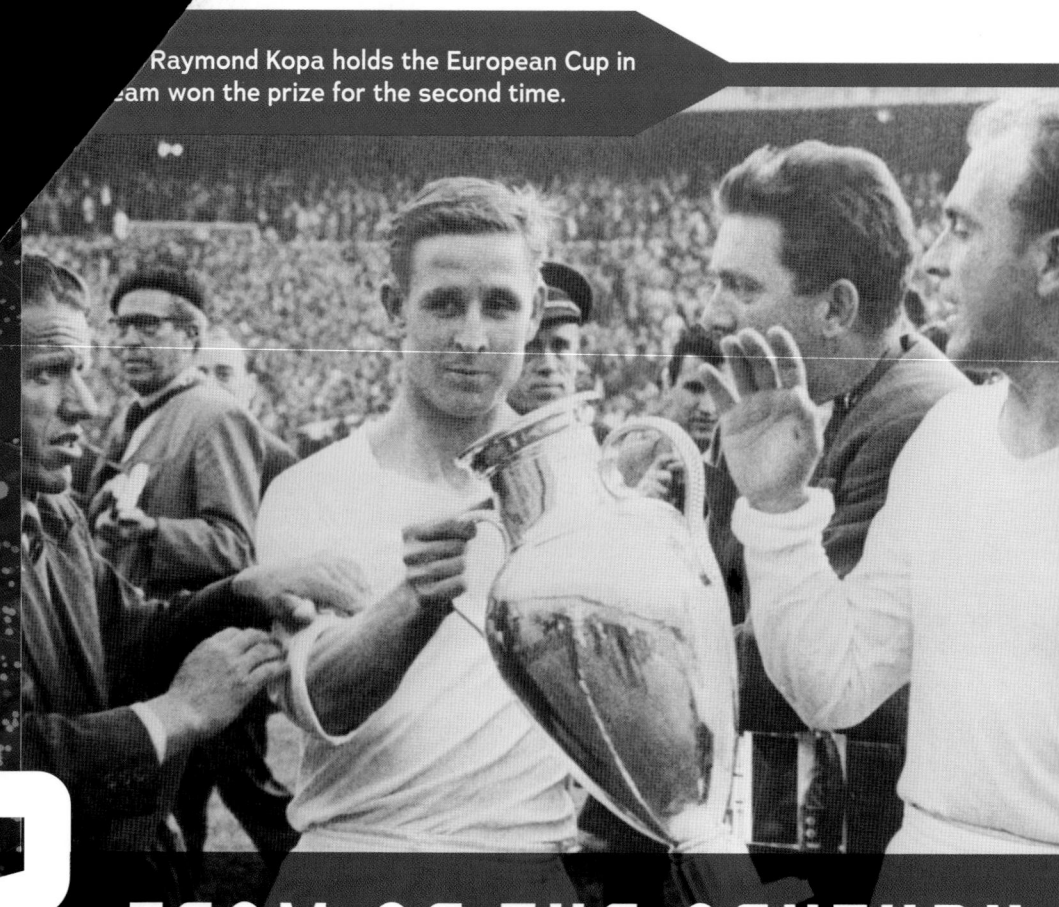

Raymond Kopa holds the European Cup in _am won the prize for the second time.

2 TEAM OF THE CENTURY

In 1955, the Union of European Football Associations (UEFA) created the European Cup. Featuring the top 16 teams in Europe, it quickly became the continent's biggest soccer prize. Real beat three teams to reach the final match that season. In Paris, France, they fell behind Stade de Reims by two goals before coming back to win, 4–3.

The following year, Real were back in the European Cup final. The game took place at Santiago Bernabeu Stadium. About 124,000 fans packed the building. Real took out Fiorentina of Italy, 2–0, to repeat as champions. They won the next three European Cups as well.

Real Madrid won its sixth European Cup in 1966. Afterward, four players appeared in a newspaper posing like the musical group the Beatles. The band was popular around the world, including in Spain. When Real fans saw

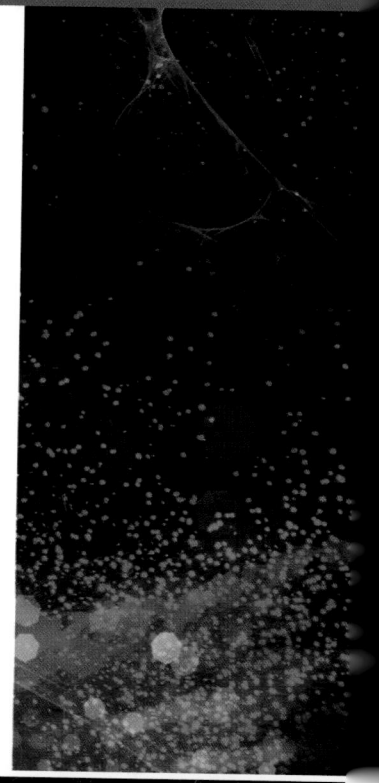

In 1960, Real Madrid won the European Cup for the fifth year in a row.

the newspaper photo, they began calling their soccer heroes the Ye-Ye team based on a Beatles song.

Real Madrid continued to capture major trophies, including the 1985 and 1986 UEFA Cup titles. The UEFA Cup is a huge tournament involving dozens of teams. A year later, they met FC Koln in the tournament's final match. Five straight goals by Real sealed the win.

In 2000, Real Madrid won the ultimate honor. FIFA, the governing body of international soccer, declared Real the world's greatest team of the 20th century.

Real Madrid won the UEFA Cup in 1985 and 1986, but the team hasn't captured the title since.

Fans know David Beckham as one of the greatest passers and shooters in soccer history.

Real kept their success going by adding some of the greatest players in the world. Zinedine Zidane, David Beckham, and others formed a group called Los Galacticos (the superstars). Real have continued to win ever since. "It is obviously great to keep adding to the trophy collection," said star Gareth Bale.

Zinedine Zidane retired from soccer in 2006 and became a successful coach.

REAL TIMELINE

1902	Three soccer players create Madrid FC.
1905	The team wins the first of four straight Copa del Rey titles.
1929	Real loses in the final match of the first La Liga season.
1947	Santiago Bernabeu Stadium opens.
1956	Real wins the first of five straight European Cups.
1985	Real wins the first of two straight UEFA Cups.
2017	Real wins the Champions League for the second straight year.

Real Madrid fans hold Spanish flags at a match in 2017.

3 ROYAL FUTURE

Santiago Bernabeu Stadium has room for more than 81,000 fans. It is full for every game. The crowd chants: "Ronaldo! Ronaldo!" The club has 68 official songs and chants.

Real Madrid is a sensation in Spain, but the team's fans are everywhere. People can join the team's official fan club to take part in lots of activities. Fan club members are called Madridistas. There are nearly one million Madridistas worldwide.

Real Madrid was the most valuable soccer team in the world in 2016. It was the fourth straight year that Real topped the list. Their worth was $3.65 billion, just ahead of rival FC Barcelona.

Santiago Bernabeu Stad
events such as rock con
addition to Real Madrid

Real's Lucas Vazquez (*right*) races ahead with the ball in 2017. Real Madrid has won more games and scored more goals than any team in European Cup history.

Real is the world's most successful soccer club. It owns a record 33 La Liga titles and 12 European Cups, as well as many other titles. It claimed four more major trophies in 2016. "We've experienced our best season, in terms of title triumphs, in our 115-year history," said team president Florentino Perez in 2016. Real Madrid's future looks truly royal.

SIDELINE REPORT

Cristiano Ronaldo is the world's highest-paid athlete. In 2017, he earned $93 million. About $35 million of that came from advertisements and other off-the-field activities.

Florentino Perez poses in front of a huge display of awards and trophies at Santiago Bernabeu Stadium in June 2017.

4 REAL MADRID

SUPER

STARS

Real Madrid's all-time roster features a long list of stars. That's exactly what you'd expect from the greatest soccer club of the 20th century. The team has excelled on the field for more than 115 years because of its great players. Read on to meet some of the best to wear Real's colors.

RICARDO ZAMORA [1930–1936]

Ricardo Zamora's nickname was the Divine One. With Real, he had two of the best La Liga seasons a goalkeeper could have. In his second and third years with the team, he allowed less than one goal per game. The Ricardo Zamora Trophy, given each year to the best goalkeeper in La Liga, is named for him.

ALFREDO DI STEFANO [1953–1964]

Many fans consider Alfredo Di Stefano to be the greatest Real player ever. A quick-striking **forward**, his nickname was the Blonde Arrow. He was the star of the team that won five straight European Cups. He received the **Ballon d'Or** award in 1957 and 1959 as the world's top player and later served two separate terms as the Real coach.

PACO GENTO [1953–1971]

Paco Gento played for Real for 18 seasons and was captain of the Ye-Ye team of the 1960s. He raced down the field at blinding speed. He won six European Cup titles, more than any other player. His 182 goals in 601 games helped Real win 12 La Liga titles.

HUGO SANCHEZ [1985–1992]

Most fans consider Hugo Sanchez to be Mexico's greatest soccer player. He starred and coached for the Mexican national team and played for 10 clubs around the world. He scored with quick strikes and was La Liga's top scorer five times. After scoring a goal, he would often celebrate by doing a front flip on the field.

ZINEDINE ZIDANE [2001—2006]

Zidane became a hero in France when he led the national team to the 1998 World Cup title. When he joined Real in 2001, the Champions League was the biggest title he hadn't won. He helped Real capture the Champions League crown the next year. He was a fierce leader on the field. "When Zidane stepped onto the **pitch**, the ten other guys just got suddenly better," said opponent Zlatan Ibrahimovic. In 2016, Zidane became Real's manager.

DAVID BECKHAM [2003—2007]

Midfielder David Beckham became a soccer superstar with England's Manchester United. He was a major celebrity and a leader of England's national team. Expectations were sky high for Beckham when he arrived in Madrid, and he delivered. He scored 20 goals with Real and helped the team capture a La Liga title.

CRISTIANO RONALDO (2009—PRESENT)

A true international superstar, Cristiano Ronaldo has earned the reputation as one of the best players. He has won the Ballon d'Or award five times and finished second five times. He is a brilliant goal scorer with more than 400 goals for Real. That's by far the most goals in team history. He also stars for Portugal's national team and is one of the richest athletes of all time.

GARETH BALE (2013—PRESENT)

In 2013, Real Madrid paid English soccer club Tottenham Hotspur more than $100 million for Gareth Bale. Then Real agreed to pay Bale about $200 million over the next six years. With so much money changing hands, the pressure was on the forward to deliver, and that's exactly what he did. Since Bale joined the team, he's led Real to three Champions League titles, La Liga and Copa del Rey crowns, and many other trophies.

STATS STORY

In 2000, Real Madrid was named the greatest soccer team of the 20th century. In the years since, they've continued to collect titles and trophies. Here are some of Real's most thrilling statistics:

MOST BALLON D'OR AWARDS BY ANY PLAYER: CRISTIANO RONALDO (5)

MOST GOALS IN TEAM HISTORY: CRISTIANO RONALDO (411)

MOST GOALS IN A SEASON: CRISTIANO RONALDO (61)

LONGEST UNBEATEN STREAK IN MAJOR COMPETITIONS: 40 GAMES (2016–2017)

LA LIGA TITLES: 33

CHAMPIONS LEAGUE TITLES: 12

SOURCE NOTES

6   "'Spectacular' Madrid Have Zidane Dancing," UEFA.com, June 4, 2017,
    http://www.uefa.com/uefachampionsleague/season=2017/matches
    /round=2000787/match=2019641/postmatch/quotes/index.html.

15 "Jose Mourinho Claims It Is 'Game Over' in Manchester United's Pursuit
    of Gareth Bale after Super Cup Defeat," *Telegraph* (London), August 8,
    2017, http://www.uefa.com/uefasupercup/season=2017/matches
    /round=2000896/match=2022539/index.html.

18 "Fans Chanting Ronaldo!," YouTube video, 0:26, posted by "Slaya,"
    January 24, 2013, https://www.youtube.com/watch?v=ilvW-TlkOY.

21 "Florentino Pérez: 'We've Experienced Our Best Season, in Terms of Title
    Triumphs, in Our 115-Year History,'" Real Madrid, January 10, 2017, http://
    www.realmadrid.com/en/news/2017/10/florentino-perez-weve-experienced
    -our-best-season-in-terms-of-title-triumphs-in-our-115-year-history.

26 Ifreke Inyang, "'Messi Plays as If He's on Playstation, Zidane Made Other
    Players Look Good'—Ibrahimovic," *Daily Post* (Nigeria), December 19, 2012,
    http://dailypost.ng/2012/12/19/messi-plays-hes-playstation-zidane-made
    -players-look-good-ibrahimovic.

GLOSSARY

Ballon d'Or: a yearly award given by *France Football* magazine to the best player in the world

centered: passed to the middle of the field near the goal

Champions League: a yearly competition among Europe's best teams

dynasty: a powerful team that wins several championships in a short period

forward: a soccer player who is responsible for scoring goals

La Liga: Spain's top soccer league

midfielder: a soccer player who usually stays in the middle of the field between the forwards and the defenders

pitch: a soccer field

rivalry: a fierce and long-lasting competition between two teams

FURTHER INFORMATION

Doeden, Matt. *Cristiano Ronaldo*. Minneapolis: Lerner Publications, 2017.

Jökulsson, Illugi. *Real Madrid: The Most Successful Club in the World*. New York: Abbeville, 2014.

Real Madrid
https://www.realmadrid.com/en

Sports Illustrated Kids: Soccer
https://www.sikids.com/soccer

UEFA: The Official Website for European Football
http://www.uefa.com

Whiting, Jim. *FC Barcelona*. Mankato, MN: Creative Education, 2017.

INDEX

PHOTO ACKNOWLEDGMENTS

The images in this book are used with the permission of: design elements: Lawkeeper/Shutterstock.com; sakkmesterke/Shutterstock.com; Michal Zduniak/Shutterstock.com; somchaij/Shutterstock.com; content: Kevin Barnes/CameraSport/Getty Images, p. 4; Valerio Pennicino/UEFA/Getty Images, p. 5; PIERRE-PHILIPPE MARCOU/AFP/Getty Images, p. 6; Burak Akbulut/Anadolu Agency/Getty Images, p. 7; The LIFE Picture Collection/Getty Images, p. 8; Wikimedia Commons (public domain), p. 9; Bob Thomas/Popperfoto/Getty Images, p. 10; Universal History Archive/UIG/Getty Images, p. 11; STAFF/AFP/Getty Images, p. 12; Mirrorpix/Collection/Newscom, p. 13; Bob Thomas/Getty Images, p. 14; Victor Fraile/Icon Sport/Getty Images, p. 15; Hiroki Watanabe/Getty Images, p. 16; GABRIEL BOUYS/AFP/Getty Images, p. 18; Power Sport Images/Getty Images, pp. 19, 20; Angel Martinez/Real Madrid/Getty Images, p. 21; EFKS/Shutterstock.com, pp. 22–23; Francis M. R. Hudson/Hulton Archive/Getty Images, p. 24 (top); Keystone-France/Gamma-Keystone/Getty Images, p. 24 (bottom); Gianni Ferrari/Getty Images, p. 25 (top); Neal Simpson/EMPICS/Getty Images, p. 25 (bottom); Team 2 Sportphoto/ullstein bild/Getty Images, p. 26 (top); Maxisport/Shutterstock.com, p. 26 (bottom); Oleh Dubyna/Shutterstock.com, p. 27 (top); Marcos Mesa Sam Wordley/Shutterstock.com, p. 27 (bottom).

Front cover: Angel Martinez/Real Madrid/Getty Images; Marcos Mesa Sam Wordley/Shutterstock.com; Oleh Dubyna/Shutterstock.com.